The Tempest

An Opera in Three Acts

Libretto by
MEREDITH OAKES
after William Shakespeare

Set to music by
THOMAS ADÈS

FABER *ff* MUSIC

Libretto © 2004 by Meredith Oakes
All rights administered worldwide by Faber Music Ltd
First published in 2004 by Faber Music Ltd
3 Queen Square London WC1N 3AU
Printed in England by Caligraving Ltd

ISBN 0-571-52337-4

Commissioned by the Royal Opera House, Covent Garden

The first performance of *The Tempest* was given by
the Royal Opera House, Covent Garden, conducted by
the composer, in a production by Tom Cairns at
the Royal Opera House on 10 February 2004

Vocal score, full score and orchestral parts
available from the publishers

To buy Faber Music publications or to find out about the full range of titles
available please contact your local retailer or Faber Music sales enquiries:

Tel: +44 (0) 1279 82 89 82   Fax: +44 (0) 1279 82 89 83
sales@fabermusic.com   fabermusic.com

CHARACTERS

Prospero	*high baritone*
Ariel	*high soprano*
Caliban	*tenor*
Miranda	*mezzo-soprano*
Ferdinand	*tenor*
King	*tenor*
Antonio	*tenor*
Stefano	*bass-baritone*
Trinculo	*counter-tenor*
Sebastian	*baritone*
Gonzalo	*bass-baritone*
COURT	*SATB chorus*

The Tempest

A remote island.

ACT ONE

Scene 1: COURT, *offstage in the shipwreck*

COURT: Hell is empty
All the devils here!

Scene 2: MIRANDA *and* PROSPERO

MIRANDA: Oh father
Storm and thunder, rain and hail
Towering waves, furious gale
The ship is wrecked, it groans, it shivers
Unnatural flames run and quiver
Screams faint like seagulls mewing
Is this my father's doing?

Woe the day
Father

There, fire and storm
While here it's calm
There black as night
While here the island's bright
Father
Is this your skill?
What creatures have you killed?
Their ship is torn apart
Their cry harrows my heart
Father
Is this your art?
Woe the day

PROSPERO: Miranda
You are my care
Living on this island
What you are
You have never questioned
Now listen to your father

Fate has brought my enemies to this shore
They must suffer as I did before

I was Milan!
I was duke!
I loved seclusion
And my books
Meanwhile my brother who agreed to represent me
Plotted in his greed to overthrow me
He studied how to grant suits, how to refuse them
How to reward his lackeys, how to abuse them
He branded me incapable!
He thought me replaceable!
He went to the King of Naples!

To Naples, crude and specious
To Naples, vain and pitiless
To Naples, gaudy, great
Conniving state
Milan the fair
Milan the artful
Milan the rare
Milan the skilful
Milan my library
Milan my liberty
To Naples gross and bold
Milan was sold

MIRANDA: Milan? What's Milan?

PROSPERO: Fair Milan
Stooping stands
Robbed of grace
Dark of face
Casual sport
Of Naples venal court

Shamed, confused
Betrayed, abused

Miranda, cheated infant
Miranda, luckless innocent
Miranda, fierce the night
And black the spite
Put out to drift
No proper vessel
A rotting raft
No mast no tackle
Me and your crying self
Me and my commonwealth
Abandoned on a ship
The rats had quit!

MIRANDA: Were we so friendless?

PROSPERO: One man helped us

Good Gonzalo
Naples' counsellor
He contrived
To save our lives
He it was
Who let me keep my books
And stocked us well
When we set sail

MIRANDA: Fearful story
I'm so sorry

PROSPERO: How could this be a brother?
How could we have one mother?
Can Anthony and I
Be from one womb?
He took my limbs
And sucked my sweetness
Usurped my skin
Effaced my features
I was exhausted
I flew, I flew, I flew transporting you
To where we could await
A better fate

MIRANDA: Father, such grief
             I want to weep

             What you have told me
             Means nothing to me
             Words full of fury
             Distant and strange

             Gone from my memory
             All you describe to me
             Sullen mystery
             Dismaying rage

             Headlands for climbing
             Sand dunes for jumping
             Shallows for swimming
             All was so clear

             No gale no ravage
             No broken wreckage
             No blast no damage
             No storm no fear

             Why have you called them
             Why have you killed them
             Why have you summoned
             Such sorrow here?

PROSPERO: Where you live is kind
             Like your sheltered mind
             Good is all you know
             Sleep my child, keep it so

(MIRANDA sleeps.)

PROSPERO: Spirit, servant, come and tell
             Are they punished, Ariel?

(ARIEL appears.)

Scene 3: ARIEL *and* PROSPERO

ARIEL: Fear to the sinner
             Fire to the impure

Storm to the villain
Harm to the wrongdoer

They are harried
They are carried
To the reef
To the deep

They are blasted
They are dismasted
They are hit
They are split

They are wave-tossed
They are flame-crossed
They are found
They are drowned

Fear to the sinner
Fire to the impure
Storm to the villain
Harm to the wrongdoer

Flame to the trespasser
Dismay to the enemy
Terror to the visitor
Pain beyond remedy

Death to the transgressor
Woe beyond measure

PROSPERO: Ariel, that's enough
There's no need to be rough
They must not be harmed
I wish them only charmed
Not a hair perished
On their clothes no blemish
Retrieve them, revive them
And bring them to the island

ARIEL: Aid to the victims
Help to the helpless
Care to the stricken
Hope to the distressed

They are hurried
They are ferried
To the shore
To the cure

Balm to the injured
Peace to the targeted
Life to the inundated
Love to the hated

PROSPERO: That's my spirit
Go and do it

Safe in this harbour
My false brother
Unscathed but marked within
Shall know his sin!

The duties I ignored
Will now be made good

Oh blind men, I'll find them
My light will reach inside them

Now heal them and free them
Where I can hide and see them

ARIEL: I'll clean them and dry them
And set them on the island

(ARIEL off.)

Scene 4: CALIBAN *and* PROSPERO (MIRANDA *asleep)*

CALIBAN: Sorcerer, die

PROSPERO: Caliban, why?

CALIBAN: Such rain
It fell like thunder
Such flame
It hissed like water
Tell me how

PROSPERO:	Caliban, not now
CALIBAN:	How you burned the vessel How you destroyed the people
PROSPERO:	Don't ask questions, slave Know your place
CALIBAN:	This island's mine I am king Yet you treat me like nothing Your art makes me bow to you As fires burn and winds blow for you I took you for my brother The island's mine, by Sycorax my mother
	When I first found you, you were weak Crouched by a rock, your child in your cloak
	I came to save you I was your friend Nor were you ever Unkind to me then You scorn me and you strike me You say you do not like me I showed you all the island The fertile and the barren All I had you were given But now you have forgotten
PROSPERO:	You lie, you whine You waste my time
CALIBAN:	You are ungrateful So is your child Miranda who used to Sleep by my side So small she was and slender Her skin was soft and tender She'd ride upon my shoulders I watched her growing older Soon she'll be having children Yes, she'll make little Calibans

PROSPERO: Abhorrent slave
             Go to your cave
             Lunatic, all this is in your mind
             Hagseed, I warn you
             I've seen you
             With Miranda
             Creeping round her
             Serpent
             I'm patient
             But if you loiter
             Near my daughter
             Filth that you are
             You devil's spawn
             I'll send you pains
             That rack your bones

(CALIBAN off.)

             Ariel

(ARIEL appears.)

ARIEL: Sir?

Scene 5: PROSPERO *and* ARIEL *(*MIRANDA *asleep)*

PROSPERO: Have you recovered them? Are they here?

ARIEL: They are sleeping
             They are dreaming
             By the shore
             All restored

             Where the parrots
             Shriek and chatter
             In the shade
             They are laid

             I have stitched them
             I have sewn them
             They are healed
             They are whole

PROSPERO: Now sing to one
            Thieving Naples' son
            Prince Ferdinand
            Heir to Milan
            Bring him here with a beckoning round
            My foes shall mourn and his grieving father
                think him drowned

ARIEL: Shall I be paid?

PROSPERO: Paid?

ARIEL: My wage

PROSPERO: Dare you ask it?

ARIEL: I do
            It's due!
            My release
            You swore
            Your promise!
            My reward
            My fee, my ransom, my freedom

PROSPERO: Fickle spirit
            So cold so prompt
            I need you yet
            Is this your thanks?
            I still have tasks
            You can't leave me

ARIEL: Eager and faithful
            Patient and true
            Zealous and cheerful
            Servant to you
            Twelve years your slave
            Soon to be free
            Oh how I crave
            My liberty

PROSPERO: Twelve years for insolence
            You were confined
            By the witch Sycorax
            In a forked pine

Sycorax died
Lest you forget
Left you inside
I prised you out

ARIEL: I have been captive
With you twelve years
I must be active
In higher spheres
Spirits must rise
Or atrophy
I only thrive
In liberty!

PROSPERO: You made a promise
When you were freed
Twelve years of service
Do as I need
Or you'll be stuck
Malignant thing
Twelve years in an oak
I'll clip your wings!

ARIEL: Eager and faithful
Patient and true
Zealous and cheerful
Servant to you
Twelve years your slave
Soon to be free
I only thrive
In liberty
I have been captive
With you twelve years
I must be active
In higher spheres
Spirits must rise
Or atrophy
I o–

PROSPERO: You made a promise
When you were freed
Twelve years of service
Do as I need

	Or you'll be stuck
	Malignant thing
	Twelve years in an oak
	Bring me Ferdinand! Sing!

ARIEL: Five fathoms deep
            Your father lies
            Those are pearls
            That were his eyes
            Nothing of him
            That was mortal
            Is the same
            His bones are coral
            He has suffered
            A sea change
            Into something
            Rich and strange
            Sea-nymphs hourly
            Ring his knell
            I can hear them
            Ding dong bell

(ARIEL and PROSPERO hide, leaving MIRANDA sleeping, as FERDINAND enters.)

Scene 6: FERDINAND *and* MIRANDA, *with* PROSPERO *and* ARIEL *unseen.*

FERDINAND: As I sat weeping
            I heard singing
            A song that pictured
            My drowned father

            This sound has calmed the storm
            And lulled the tempest's rage
            Has put the winds to sleep
            And smoothed the pounding waves

            This influence, this hush
            Across the water stealing
            Has stopped the thunder's noise
            And stilled my weeping

Who's here?
Wondrous
Is she
A goddess?

MIRANDA: *(waking)* Are you a spirit?
Are you a shade?
Are you a thing my father made?

PROSPERO: *(aside)* She's awake
Did my spell break?

MIRANDA: You're handsome
Are you human?

FERDINAND: Here on the coast
A ship was lost
I'm all that's left
The rest are dead

MIRANDA: I never knew
A man could look like you

FERDINAND: Am I so strange?

MIRANDA: No don't change

PROSPERO: *(aside)* What next
She's bewitched!

FERDINAND: I never saw
Your like before

MIRANDA: I never saw
Your like before
You're wet through
Let me tend you

FERDINAND: I never saw your equal
I'll make you Queen of Naples

(PROSPERO appears to FERDINAND and MIRANDA.)

PROSPERO: Sir, Naples unseated me
Took my sovereignty
My dukedom
Stolen by treason

This was the crime
Between your house and mine

FERDINAND: Sir you're angry
Sir I'm sorry
I came here
From Naples
My father
Was king there
I'm lost sir
Is this your daughter?

PROSPERO: Stupid youth
What's the use?
You're not here
To gawp at her
Young fool
Be still!

(PROSPERO immobilises FERDINAND.)

MIRANDA: Father don't oh father please
Try to put him at his ease

FERDINAND: I'm paralysed by him
I can't command my limbs!

MIRANDA: Why must you be so savage?
He's not done you any damage

FERDINAND: He has practised
Some trick, some magic

PROSPERO: Try to understand
This is Ferdinand
Gilded and handsome
Through our misfortune
Nurtured on the squalor
Of his odious father
Raised in a kingdom
Of thieves and villains

MIRANDA: Father look at him!
How can you say such things?

FERDINAND: In what dream am I bound?
Am I lost or am I found?

MIRANDA: Never think that I'll forgive you
Let him go, or I won't love you!
What will he think?
Why have you done this?
Why do you hate him?
What twisted reason?

FERDINAND: Though he's full of hate
I don't fear his threats
Or persecution
I don't fear this prison

No, prison will be sweet
I will stand and wait
Nothing will dismay me
If she is near me

MIRANDA: Oh such rage
You're so brave
Such fury
How could he
No, it's not true
Father shame on you
Nothing you can say
Threaten as you may
Will ever change me
If he is near me

PROSPERO: He's unworthy of you
You don't know your value
Leave this child of sin
I must punish him
And the rest as well
Bring me to them, Ariel

ARIEL: Bow-wow, bow-wow
What should I do now? bow-wow
Shall I bark, bow-wow
These mortals and their woe bow-wow
When will they let me go bow-wow

ACT TWO

Scene 1: *The* COURT *on the island, with* STEFANO, TRINCULO,
ANTONIO, SEBASTIAN, GONZALO *and* THE KING OF
NAPLES, *and with* PROSPERO *and* ARIEL *unseen.*

COURT: Alive, awake
      In some place
      Where the storm
      Has left no trace

      Gull tracks
      Tide wrack
      Glistening shells
      Flotsam, kelp

      Woodland
      Dry sand
      No rain
      Tranquil, strange

      Gashes
      Vanished
      Clothes untorn
      As if newborn

      Is it possible?
      Is it a miracle?

      Shining beaches
      Shimmering hills
      Tangled branches
      Where something dwells

      Fleeting
      Leaping
      Whispering
      Some unseen thing

STEFANO: I had the notion
      I flew above the ocean

STEFANO *and* TRINCULO:
      Like some gull
      Hard to tell

TRINCULO: Dragons were coiling
Cauldrons were boiling
Above my head

STEFANO *and* TRINCULO:
We might be dead

STEFANO: We were sunk

TRINCULO: I was drunk

STEFANO: I had a skinful

TRINCULO: I clung to a barrel

STEFANO: No blood no bruise

STEFANO *and* TRINCULO:
All smooth

COURT: In what tempest were we blown?
To what coast have we come?

(PROSPERO and ARIEL enter unseen.)

PROSPERO: Now I see them
All together
There's Naples' king!
With his brother
There's Gonzalo
Once my saviour
There he is
There's my brother

Taunt them, haunt them
Goad and tease
Prick them, trick them
Give them no peace

ARIEL: Taunt them, haunt them
Goad and tease
Prick them, trick them

(PROSPERO turns away.)

ANTONIO: All safe on land

SEBASTIAN: All save Ferdinand

COURT:	He's not here Naples' son The king's in tears
GONZALO:	(*to THE KING*) Sir, be cheerful This is remarkable! Please don't weep Your Majesty Plucked from the storm Our clothes fresh, as if unworn! Sir, this is evidence We are loved by Providence! Prince Ferdinand your son Is surely in good hands
TRINCULO:	Lord Gonzalo
STEFANO:	Hopeful fellow
ANTONIO:	(*to THE KING*) Sir, I saw him in the water Striking bravely for the land The prince is an outstanding swimmer! I've every confidence in that young man
ARIEL:	(*in SEBASTIAN's voice*) Liar
ANTONIO:	What's that, sire?
SEBASTIAN:	I didn't speak
ANTONIO:	My mistake (*to THE KING*) Sir, the tempest has not claimed him He's loved by fate! He is your son He's energetic and determined A prince if ever there was one
ARIEL:	(*in SEBASTIAN's voice*) Shameless
ANTONIO:	(*to SEBASTIAN*) What, your Highness?
SEBASTIAN:	I've not spoken
ANTONIO:	Sir, you're joking
SEBASTIAN:	You're disturbed
ANTONIO:	No, I heard

SEBASTIAN: Milan, your vanity, your self-promotion
Have brought us to this godforsaken shore
For you we braved the perils of the ocean
The ship is wrecked, my nephew is no more

ANTONIO: Prince Sebastian, as your host
I did my best
Bringing you away
On holiday

I don't deserve
Your hurtful words
My only thought
Was for the court

SEBASTIAN: My brother's only child, flower of the nation
How will you bring him back? What will you do?
We came from Naples at your invitation
The blame for this misfortune lies with you

ANTONIO: I wanted everything
Perfect for the king
The hurricane
Was unforeseen

SEBASTIAN: Spare us your excuses
They're quite useless

THE KING OF NAPLES:
Oh Prince of Naples and Milan
What fish has made its meal on you!
Oh hear me Ferdinand
I should have died not you

ANTONIO: He's not drowned
He'll be found!
Courage sir, and rule!

ARIEL: *(in ANTONIO's voice)* Feeble fool

SEBASTIAN: He slights my brother

ANTONIO: Not me, some other!

COURT: What did he say?
Traitor, you'll pay

ANTONIO:	How dare you turn against me
	With abuse and strictures
	You queued up to befriend me
	You posed with me for pictures!

Your courtly entertainments
Were paid for with my purse
Milan was patron
To volumes of your verse

Your feasts your palaces
Your pleasures and your pets
Your schemes your businesses
I guaranteed your debts

COURT:	It's all his fault
	And still he talks
	His disrespect
	Is manifest

| ANTONIO: | I invited you to dinner |

| ARIEL: | (in ANTONIO's voice) Wasters, idlers, thieves and sinners |

COURT:	Hark at him, hark at him
	Now he's unmasked
	Ungrateful trash
	He should be thrashed!

| ANTONIO: | Friends, desist |
| | We're bewitched! |

COURT:	Obnoxious man
	Charlatan
	Impudent vermin
	He should be beaten

| ANTONIO: | Wait, good people! |

| COURT: | Thrash him, charlatan |
| | Thrash him |

| SEBASTIAN: | At him, Naples! |

| COURT: | Beat him |
| | At him, Naples |

(CALIBAN enters.)

Scene 2: *As before, with* CALIBAN

COURT:	A monster! A local!
CALIBAN:	These are visitors These are voyagers With jewelled hands
COURT:	He mumbles! He gestures
CALIBAN:	From some bright land
COURT:	What's he trying to tell us?
CALIBAN:	Dressed like royalty
COURT:	He likes us
CALIBAN:	How they stare at me
COURT:	He speaks gently
CALIBAN:	Mysterious grace In every face
COURT:	He's ugly He's friendly
CALIBAN:	Such men such women You have dropped from heaven
SEBASTIAN:	Yes, savage loon We're from the moon
STEFANO:	A credulous monster
TRINCULO:	A weak besotted creature

STEFANO *and* TRINCULO:

Monster will you help us?
You've so much to teach us
How to plait our hair with mud
How to be pigeon-footed
How to gaze with gaping mouth
Wild vague and stupid

What shall we give you
To show how much we love you
Buttons or handkerchiefs
Braid from our coatsleeves
Pieces of petty change
Or some brandy?
We've got some handy

CALIBAN: This is a sign
You are kind

TRINCULO: Just help yourself
Drink all you want

STEFANO: It's vintage from
The royal vault

(CALIBAN *drinks*.)

GONZALO: The creature's
Not used to liquor
Is it prudent
To tempt him to it?

CALIBAN: Oh brotherhood
This drink is good

I'll take you where mud crabs grow
I'll show you a jay's nest
I'll lead you where the best springs flow
I'll help you snare the marmoset
With my long nails I'll dig you pignuts
I'll swim to catch you turtles
I'll fetch you clustering chestnuts
From the rocks get you young scamels

(CALIBAN *drinks*.)

SOLOISTS: He babbles

COURT: What are scamels?

CALIBAN: Oh potent drink
That makes me strong

STEFANO, TRINCULO *and* COURT:
        Yes, have some more!
        That's right, go on!

CALIBAN: It burns in me

COURT: It burns in him

CALIBAN: With tongues of fire

COURT: With tongues of fire

CALIBAN: It lifts me up

COURT: It lifts him up

CALIBAN: Higher and higher

COURT: Higher and higher

ARIEL: Higher and higher

COURT: Who's there?

ARIEL: Who's there?

COURT: It's air!

ARIEL: It's air!

STEFANO, TRINCULO, ANTONIO, SEBASTIAN *and* COURT:
        Haunted coast
        It's a ghost

CALIBAN: Friends don't fear
        The island's full of noises
        Sounds and voices
        It's the spirits

        Sometimes they come
        After I've slept
        And hum me
        Back to sleep
        With a twanging
        And a sweetness
        Like playing
        A thousand instruments

Then I dream
I'm seeing heaven
It's as if
The clouds had opened

I see riches
Raining from them
Then I wake
And cry to dream again

COURT: Spirits he calls them
What is this island?

GONZALO: (*to CALIBAN*) Sir, what you're saying I don't know
Nor where we are nor where to go
There was a tempest not long since
Can you help us find our prince?

CALIBAN: No such storm have I seen
Since my mother Sycorax was queen
She could enrage the tide
She could make the toadfish hide
She could call demons here
That shook the coast with fear
Her art was nothing though
To the art my master knows

ANTONIO: So we're not alone here!

CALIBAN: I was a child
In his hands
By treachery
He took my lands

He killed your prince!
He made the storm
He means you harm
He hates you all

ANTONIO: Do you hear, gentlemen
What he says of sorcery?
Certain scholars have been known
To perform prodigies

	Who are we to dismiss What the simple creature says? How do we know what arts May be practised in this place?
CALIBAN:	He can summon up at will Suns, moons, heats, chills
COURT:	No-one can tell what is real
CALIBAN:	Changing clouds to galleons Peopling the empty shore with companions He makes you believe You see and hear and touch what he conceives No stronger art I know Than the art of Prosper–

(PROSPERO punishes CALIBAN.)

ANTONIO:	Monster Who's your master?
CALIBAN:	I can't tell I'm not well
SEBASTIAN:	*(to ANTONIO)* The creature's drunk And you're a crank Keep your theories To yourself You've done enough! Spreading groundless fear among us Magnifies the wrong you've done us No more currency is left you You've already killed my nephew
GONZALO:	The monster Speaks wild nonsense We'll find the prince Although the jungle's dense We'll go on trying We'll search the island We'll not fear Whatever's here It will be done We'll find your son

COURT: We'll go on trying
            We'll search the island
            We'll not fear
            Whatever's here
            It will be done
            We'll find your son

GONZALO: We'll press ahead –

THE KING OF NAPLES:
            My son is dead

            The sea mocks
            Our search on land
            He's lost
            Whom we stray to find
            Vain
            He's gone

            Words, words, words
            Can't cure it
            As for hope
            I'll not endure it
            The pain's
            Too keen

            Would I were bedded
            Where Ferdinand lies
            Yes mudded
            In that ooze
            Oh
            Let him go

GONZALO: Sir, he's not gone
            We'll find him further on

(The KING OF NAPLES is led off by the COURT and GONZALO. ARIEL goes with them. CALIBAN, STEFANO and TRINCULO remain, with PROSPERO aside.)

PROSPERO: Go and search
            Where there's no path
            Go in circles
            Drink the salt marsh
            Wander the swamp

Stumble and crawl
Babble and rave
Go till you fall
Driven insane
You'll know my name

(PROSPERO off.)

Scene 3: CALIBAN, STEFANO *and* TRINCULO

STEFANO: They won't find him
            He's a dead man
            It's a tragedy

TRINCULO: Have a brandy

STEFANO: Marooned
            We're all doomed
            No food no cover

TRINCULO: Have another

STEFANO: Lost in the wilderness
            That it should come to this

TRINCULO: There's always hope, I always think
            Have a drink

STEFANO: Naples, goodbye
            Here's where we'll die

CALIBAN: All your woe
            Comes from my foe

STEFANO: What's that, monster?

TRINCULO: Is his fit over?

CALIBAN: Help me regain my land
            I'll be your friend

STEFANO: Oh certainly

TRINCULO: Thanks, your majesty

CALIBAN: When he's dead
            You'll be king instead

	You'll be master
	Of his daughter
STEFANO:	Is she clean?
CALIBAN:	She'll be your queen
TRINCULO:	Is she sweet?
CALIBAN:	She visits my sleep
	Soft as the dew

STEFANO *and* TRINCULO:
> We'll go with you

STEFANO:
> The mage will die
> And on his child
> I'll sire a nation
> In the wild
>
> Thought is free
> And in this land
> I'll bow no more
> To any man

TRINCULO:
> The mage will die
> And on his child
> We'll sire a nation
> In the wild
>
> Thought is free
> And in this land
> We'll bow no more
> To any man

CALIBAN:
> The mage will die
> And on his child
> You'll sire a nation
> In the wild
>
> Thought is free
> And in this land
> You'll bow no more
> To any man

(CALIBAN, STEFANO and TRINCULO off.)

Scene 4: FERDINAND, *then* MIRANDA, *then* PROSPERO *unseen.*

FERDINAND: What was before
Is no more
My father's gone
I live on
Bound and tied
Till I die
Trees and stones
To be my home

Lost like a dream
All that's been
Nothing left
But this grief
Only she
Comforts me
In this night
She is the light

(MIRANDA enters.)

MIRANDA: How can I offer
What I'd give?
How can I ask for
What I'd have?

Do you love me?
Why do I weep?
Love is strong
I am weak

FERDINAND: As soon as I saw you
My heart flew to serve you

As if it had waited
My whole life to love you

(PROSPERO enters unseen.)

What's your name?

MIRANDA: Miranda

I've disobeyed
Father said not to say

FERDINAND: Admired Miranda
            Wonder of my life
            My wife

(MIRANDA frees FERDINAND.)

MIRANDA *and* FERDINAND:
            High on the headland
            Low in the dry sand
            Deep in the woodland
            There we'll lie

            Or on a rock face
            Near where the waves break
            Hearing the tide race
            You and I

            Oh will you have me
            Tell me you love me
            If you are with me
            I am entire

            My lover smiling
            Blessed asylum
            Bountiful island
            All I desire

(MIRANDA and FERDINAND off.)

PROSPERO: Miranda
            I've lost her
            I cannot rule their minds
            My child has conquered me
            A stronger power than mine
            Has set the young man free

ACT THREE

Scene 1: CALIBAN, STEFANO *and* TRINCULO, *all drunk.*

CALIBAN: This way
                They're close by

TRINCULO: Wait a moment
                For refreshments

STEFANO: Monster, have mercy
                I'm thirsty

TRINCULO: So am I

CALIBAN: It's not much further
                Death to her father

STEFANO *and* TRINCULO:
                One more drink

CALIBAN: Yes, but be quick

                I drink to a man
                King Stefan
                A glorious reign will soon begin
                King Stephen with his maiden queen

STEFANO: Run girl and hide
                I'll come to you
                I'll show you what
                A man can do

TRINCULO: Run girl and hide
                He'll come to you
                He'll show you what
                A man can do

CALIBAN: Quiet or we'll be found

STEFANO *and* TRINCULO:
                One more round
                A glorious reign will soon begin
                King Stephen with his maiden queen

CALIBAN:	(aside) By my art you are deceived
	Do your part, I'll be free
ALL:	Death to her father

(Off.)

Scene 2: PROSPERO *and* ARIEL, *then* COURT

PROSPERO:	Spirit must I right my wrongs?
	Miranda's gone
	Are you faithful, Ariel?
	Oh serve me well

ARIEL:	By rotting ponds
	By dripping cliffs
	In sinking ground
	I've led them up and down
	Through sucking quicksand
	Through swamps and saltpans
	Through weeping leaves
	Past the stinging tree
	Through swarms of flies
	Oh let me rise
	I've chased them high and low
	Oh let me go!

PROSPERO:	No
	Don't betray me
	Spirit don't fail me
	Are they dismayed?
	What do they say?
	Do they see?
	Have they thought of me?

ARIEL:	See them
	They are weak
	They can hardly walk!

(COURT *enters including* THE KING OF NAPLES, GONZALO, ANTONIO *and* SEBASTIAN.)

COURT:	The island is a maze of straight paths and meanders We'll all die If the prince escaped the tempest's anger He's fallen prey to some animal's hunger
GONZALO:	My old bones ache I can walk no further
COURT:	We'll all die here before much longer
SEBASTIAN:	(*to* GONZALO) Fool You've tired us out And in vain I knew it was a waste of time
THE KING OF NAPLES:	Ferdinand, why did the sea Take you not me? Or some other My brother You were young You were fair Now Sebastian is my heir Soon this grief will end my life Ferdinand I'll not let Naples forget My brother lacks your merit He'll not inherit Gonzalo heed me You'll succeed me I'll see to it You will be regent
GONZALO:	You're tired sir Sleep sir So weary so heavy

(*All sleep except* ANTONIO *and* SEBASTIAN, PROSPERO *and* ARIEL *watching.*)

ANTONIO:	You're not your brother's favourite
SEBASTIAN:	That's no secret
ANTONIO:	All of a sudden They're sleeping

This accident could make us friends
One day we'll see Naples again

SEBASTIAN: Say what you like
Laugh at my fall
I can expect
Nothing at all

ANTONIO: That's up to you
You must decide
See how they sleep
As if they'd died

If it were so
You'd be the king
None of the court
Could say a thing

SEBASTIAN: You have strange thoughts
Just like my own
You had a brother
Then he was gone

ANTONIO *and* SEBASTIAN:
Dare and succeed
Do it my soul
Fortune, it's said
Waits on the bold

One for the king
One for this lord
Two at one blow
Put to the sword

ARIEL: Open your eyes if you value your lives
Oh see what's stirring
Old men stop your snoring

GONZALO *and* COURT:
(waking) Murder!

KING: *(waking)* What's that shout?

ANTONIO: Someone's about

SEBASTIAN: Strangers

ANTONIO *and* SEBASTIAN:
　　　　　We armed ourselves against the danger

PROSPERO:　　They're the same, still the same
　　　　　As if nothing had changed
　　　　　Poison to the core
　　　　　Malevolent as before
　　　　　What suff'ring will move them?
　　　　　Are these creatures human?

　　　　　My art must strike their hearts

(*ARIEL makes a musical sound. ARIEL causes a feast to appear.*)

COURT:　　　Help us!
　　　　　What things are these?
　　　　　Bizarre beyond belief
　　　　　Strange vision

SEBASTIAN *and* COURT:
　　　　　It's provisions

GONZALO:　　Friends, we've been given
　　　　　Food from heaven

　　　　　If I were king
　　　　　Of such a land as this
　　　　　All men would live
　　　　　In idleness

　　　　　No rich, no poor
　　　　　Service would be unknown
　　　　　No writ no law
　　　　　No business, none

　　　　　No knife no gun
　　　　　No crime no felony
　　　　　No need of engines
　　　　　No usury

　　　　　No trade there'd be
　　　　　No gold no sin
　　　　　There'd be no sovereign –

ANTONIO:　　If he were king

SEBASTIAN: So much for politics
               Let's eat

*(They take food. Thunder, lightning, ARIEL like a harpy flaps his wings
on the tables and the feast vanishes or turns to something horrible.)*

ALL: Fearful creature

ARIEL: *(as a harpy)* You are men of sin
               As you know
               You from Milan
               Banished Prospero

               Even the hungry sea
               Could not stomach you
               But belched you up
               Remembering Prospero

               As you sentenced them
               Twelve years ago
               To starve and die
               The child and Prospero

               You are sentenced here
               To wasting slow
               Extinction like your
               Brother Prospero

SEBASTIAN, GONZALO *and* COURT:
               This is heaven's anger

(COURT and SEBASTIAN run off.)

THE KING OF NAPLES *and* ANTONIO:
               Monstrous monstrous

ANTONIO: I heard his voice, I saw his face

THE KING *and* ANTONIO:
               Prospero is in this place

               Monstrous monstrous on the shore
               Prospero in the ocean's roar

ANTONIO: Prospero's ghost condemns me

THE KING: Nature speaks against me

ANTONIO: My mind's undone

THE KING: My sin has killed my son!

(THE KING and ANTONIO run off in distraction.)

GONZALO: What they did long ago
             Has come back to them now
             Poison from buried crimes
             Has worked upon their minds

(GONZALO goes off after THE KING and ANTONIO. PROSPERO and ARIEL remain.)

PROSPERO: Their brains are boiled within their skulls
             Spirit this is magical

             Souls in torment make your payment
             Now they dwell with me in hell

             With my art I've dimmed the sun
             Made the wild ocean run
             Broken Jove's stout oak
             With fire from his own bolt
             The headland I've shaken
             I've made the dead waken
             And brought hell's fury to the shore
             Nothing more

(MIRANDA and FERDINAND enter.)

Scene 3: MIRANDA, FERDINAND, PROSPERO, *then* CALIBAN *with* STEFANO *and* TRINCULO

MIRANDA: Father
             Ferdinand and I –

FERDINAND: Sir, she's my bride

PROSPERO: My life's work
             Is nothingness
             I shall never
             Know your bliss

MIRANDA: Father don't be angry
I'm so happy

PROSPERO: Miranda forgive your father
My work was hard
The end is harder
To wish you well here's Ariel

(ARIEL appears.)

FERDINAND: Is it a spirit?

PROSPERO: Yes
My servant

FERDINAND: Awesome parent

ARIEL: Children born of mortal strife
May you live a happy life
Prospero's revenge is done
Naples soon will see his son

FERDINAND: My father? Alive?

PROSPERO: Naples survived

ARIEL: Fly away from these sad times
Rise above your fathers' crimes

FERDINAND: When can I see him?

PROSPERO: Soon you'll greet him

ARIEL: Prospero has had his vengeance
Prospero who made the tempest

FERDINAND: Sir I don't understand

PROSPERO: Wait! I smell Caliban

FERDINAND: The tempest? You sent it?

PROSPERO: Our revels are ended

(PROSPERO makes ARIEL vanish.)

Why do you stare?
He's melted into air

So cities will perish
Palaces vanish
The globe itself
Dissolve
Nothing stay
All will fade

(*CALIBAN enters with STEFANO and TRINCULO.*)

CALIBAN: Murder this man
I am Caliban
Punish his crime
The island's mine

Caliban's reign will soon begin
King Caliban with his maiden queen

PROSPERO, STEFANO, TRINCULO:
Caliban
Have you gone mad?

CALIBAN: Give me your daughter
We'll have Calibans
Many and strong
So my line goes on
She was promised
Raised from childhood
To be my queen
Give her to me

PROSPERO: Wretch
Have you seen yourself?

Have you thought of my daughter's honour
Burdened with such a husband

MIRANDA: You're always following
Always watching
When I walk the beach
Or the path on the cliffs
Always there
Alien, near
You and me
How could that be?

(MIRANDA and FERDINAND off.)

PROSPERO: Poor beast
Last in the race
Creature
You have no future

(PROSPERO makes ARIEL appear and CALIBAN, STEFANO and TRINCULO vanish.)

PROSPERO: Ariel, one thing
The king

ARIEL: He and your brother
Stare and shudder
Their minds are lost
In fear and horror
While Gonzalo's tears
Run down his beard
Your spell so works them
That if you saw them
Your heart would soften
Mine would, were I human

PROSPERO: If you who are air
Feel their trouble
So much the more
Shall I be merciful

This hour your work will cease
You'll be released

(ANTONIO and THE KING OF NAPLES enter, distracted, followed by GONZALO.)

Scene 4: EVERYONE, *eventually, except* CALIBAN

PROSPERO: Quietness will comfort
Wits that have suffered

Waken madmen
Your eyes are opened
My name you know
Prospero

ANTONIO: *(coming to his senses)* Prospero living
I thought I'd killed him

THE KING OF NAPLES:
(coming to his senses) Your pulse beats
You're flesh and blood
I fear
I've been mad
Forgive what I did
My son is dead

I'll do anything you ask me
Only please show me his body
My sins have brought this sorrow on me

Take back your dukedom

PROSPERO: I'll give you more than your kingdom

(PROSPERO reveals MIRANDA and FERDINAND.)

GONZALO: The prince!

THE KING: Oh providence!
Are you real
It's not my eyes
I couldn't bear to lose you twice
Ferdinand embrace your father

PROSPERO: This is my child Miranda

THE KING: O heaven's mercy

FERDINAND: Father, we're married

THE KING: From my daughter
I the father
Like an infant
Plead forgiveness

MIRANDA: How good they are, how bright, how grand
And I am loved by Ferdinand

FERDINAND: Oh perfection of my life
I've a father and a wife

PROSPERO: Now my work is at an end
I can mar and I can mend

THE KING: Now my child is given me
              I'll abandon vanity

GONZALO: Now the wild despair is past
              Reconciled and healed at last

              How these things happened who can say?
              Or how our vessel came this way

(COURT and SEBASTIAN in.)

PROSPERO: Calm your mind
              Your woes are left behind
              Your ship is new
              And waits for you

COURT: From the ocean
              Our ship which was broken
              Is risen
              The prince who was missing
              Is here and living
              Our sins are forgiven

SEBASTIAN: Salute the power of heaven

MIRANDA: Oh brave new world

PROSPERO: Oh simple girl

COURT: Who are these people
              More than strange

THE KING: This is a marriage fate arranged
              Our kingdom will be stable
              This match unites Milan and Naples

PROSPERO: Bring the other men as well
              I forgot them, Ariel

ARIEL: This task
              Is the last

(STEFANO and TRINCULO appear.)

STEFANO *and* TRINCULO:
              Are we awake?
              And in good shape?
              It seems we are

How my head aches
Oh can it be
We're going back
To Italy

COURT: Rejoice
Oh soon
We'll sail for home

GONZALO: Bless this isle
Where Prospero found his dukedom
Ferdinand his bride
And Naples Ferdinand

GONZALO *and* COURT:
You gods look down
All who were lost are found

(GONZALO, STEFANO, TRINCULO, SEBASTIAN and COURT off.)

PROSPERO: *(to THE KING)* As far as Naples I'll keep you company
We'll marry these young people with proper ceremony

THE KING: And as we travel
You'll tell me marvels

(THE KING, FERDINAND and MIRANDA off.)

ANTONIO: Fortunate pair
A state affair

PROSPERO: To call you brother I've no wish
Still I'll forgive

ANTONIO: You'll forgive at no cost
You've won I've lost

I've lost my pride my life
Your child is Naples' wife

Naples' wife, spoiled child of fortune
Which you call the will of heaven

The will of heaven which decreed
You were born better than me

Better than me with my poor courage
Which has turned to your advantage

> Your advantage blocks my breath
> And your life has been my death

(ANTONIO off.)

PROSPERO: Pride, pride
                All will die

                I'll drown my book
                I'll break my stave
                I'll rule in Milan
                Beside my grave

(PROSPERO breaks his stave as ARIEL departs.)

                Ariel
                Stay with me
                Ariel
                Save me
                Ariel
                Farewell

ARIEL: *(offstage)* A–i–e

PROSPERO: Now I've no art
                Pity take my part

(PROSPERO off. CALIBAN enters.)

Scene 5: CALIBAN, *with* ARIEL *offstage.*

CALIBAN: Who was here?
                Have they disappeared?
                Were there others?
                Were we brothers?
                Did we feast?
                And give gifts?
                Were there fires
                And ships?
                They were human seeming
                I was dreaming

                In the gleam of the sand

ARIEL:	*(offstage)* A–i–e
CALIBAN:	Caliban
	In the hiss of the spray In the deep of the bay
	In the gulf in the swell Caliban
ARIEL:	*(offstage)* A–i–e

END